Discoveries
by
Gary Beck

PURPLE UNICORN MEDIA

Published by Purple Unicorn Media

Discoveries
by Gary Beck

Copyright © 2023 by Gary Beck
All rights are reserved

Author: Gary Beck
Contact via the publisher: info@purpleunicornmedia.com

Cover image by Robin Stacey

ISBN 978-1-915692-61-0

Dedication

To R.C. A young man of geat promise who got lost, then devoured in the wilderness of cities

Contents

Wounded Land	9
Memories	10
Ceremony	11
Down in the Mines	12
Forgotten Flights	14
Tidal Flow	15
Call to Duty	16
Fraying Reason	17
Wonders of the City	18
Treasure Hunter	19
America Unfurled	20
The Park	28
Armaments	29
Continuation	30
Clinic	31
Different Customs	32
Strange Surroundings	33
After Decline	35
Whose Country is it?	36
Social Malfeasance	39
Innovation	40

O Joyous Day	41
Our Land, Lost	42
Imperial Reach	43
Democracy Wounded	44
Selfish is	46
Fake News	47
Persistence	48
Gun Crazy	50
Abandonment	51
Extinction Path	52
Park Sights	53
Know Thy Deceivers	54
Loss	55
Priorities	56
War Power	57
Replace Humans	58
Homeless in Paradise	59
Endurance	60
Madness Revealed	61
Afghan Climate	62
Tourist Drudge	63
Imprecation	64
Surfs Up	65

Triumph	66
Beach Din	67
Afghan Pullout	68
Ersatz Surfers	69
Dedicated	70
Lost Flock	71
Mega-Corp Abuse	72
Malice Aforethought	73
Ode to Texas	74
Stampede	75
War For Whom?	76
Spector Weapons	77
Audiology Department	78
Blindness	79
Ignored	80
Servitude	81
Orders	82
National Interests	83
Separate	84
Aquatic Afflictions	85
Opportunist	86
The Eyes of Texas…	87
Dimming Calls	88

Veterans Care	89
Decayed Conditions	90
Interpreter Escape	91
Big Wave Dreams	92
Politics Agonistes	93
Airborne	94
Aging	95
Failing Wings	96
Do Gooder	97
Tourist Sight	98
At Last	99
Depleted Waterway	100

Wounded Land

Children leave the school
single file,
hands over heads,
intently watched
by armed cops
looking for a shooter
concealed with the innocent,
tensions so high
one accidental move
might make an intense cop
open fire.

Memories

When I was a young girl
my family went to New Smyrna Beach,
a small, sleepy Florida beach town
for much of the long winter.
I walked the beach
collecting sea shells.
Sometimes I found a conch,
brought it to my ear,
listened to the eerie sound
of the ocean
and didn't return it to the sea.
Now that I am old
my grandchildren and I
still visit New Smyrna beach
that now teems with tourists.
We walk the beach
but there are no shells.
When I tell them that once
there were flocks of shorebirds
they pretend to listen,
but their thumbs are busy
texting their friends.

Ceremony

I sit in comfort
in the luxurious house
of a former member
of the Afghan government
finally defeated
by the holy warriors
of the true faith.
I watch the CNN news
as the Americans
carry out the coffins
of the Marines who died
in the suicide bombing
near the Kabul airport.
The President Biden
and other officials
military and civilian
watch respectfully
as the solemn Marines
carry the coffins
of their comrades
to the waiting trucks
that will take them
to a place of honored rest,
not like my brothers
who died in battle
and did not need
earthly recognition
for their sacrifice
against infidel invaders,
since they are at peace
in the bosom of Allah.

Down in the Mines

Coal miners lead dangerous lives
going down in the deep hole
where Mother Earth waits
to swallow intruders.
Conditions have slightly improved
from oppressed times
when armed guards kept miners in line,
who were paid in company scrip,
with pay docked for costs of housing,
medical care, tools used in the mines,
while union organizers
were beaten, jailed, assassinated
and families were indebted
to the company store.

When miners resisted
almost indentured servitude
they were fired, blacklisted,
so they couldn't find work
in other mines.
Abuses were intolerable
and the miner's protests
were violently put down
by hirelings of the bosses,
whose only concern was profits,
no matter how difficult the lives
of miners and their families,
until tired of endless suffering
the miners fought back.

Mine owners were never fair
and would never share
money earned by laborers

who lived in virtual squalor,
while the bosses lived in mansions
and would never tolerate
defiance to their rules.

But the miners were proud men,
not clerks who would melt away
before armed thugs of the bosses
and fought for their rights

in the era of mine wars,
including a great battle
when thousands of united miners
fought the sheriff's men
in the pay of the bosses,
until the U.S. Army intervened
and stopped the fighting,
with no improvements for the miners,
victims of ruthless capitalists.

Forgotten Flights

Old Grey Wing keeps telling us
of the pelicans of old
as we try to nest on the little island,
forced to fly when humans come
interrupting his tale of our fathers.
Sometimes the humans come
after dark, forcing us to fly
in the dangerous night,
some too tired at first light
to hunt for fish.
We try not to notice
those who make their last flight
and we try to ignore
old Grey Wing's tales
of flights of hundreds
in great Pelican V's,
filling the skies,
not like today
when the most we see
are flights of 8 or 9
that can't agree on a leader.

Tidal Flow

When I walk on the beach
I see the loneliness
of the Florida surfer,
who waits and waits
for the big wave
that never comes.

Call to Duty

The waiting room is empty.
The doctors and nurses
have departed.
Too tired to party
after treating the ill
for what seemed like
endless hours.
Tears, sweat, vomit, blood
flowed almost endlessly.

And the medical staff
stemmed the flow,
made repairs
as best they could,
got grateful thanks
from the healed,
hopefully went home
satisfied they served
the needs of the people.

Fraying Reason

The line for Covid-19 shots
grows longer and longer.
Teachers rush for vaccinations
to comply with the job mandate.
A small group of loud protestors
try to persuade those waiting
that it's a violation
of their constitutional rights
to be compelled to get the shots.
A man tries to convince them
it's a health issue, not rights,
but they refuse to listen,
get angry, insult him, threaten,
then attack him violently,
until others intervene
and the protestors run away,
a typical example
of the American way
of problem solving.

Wonders of the City

No matter how often
I pass familiar streets
the city is always different.
A building noticed for the first time.
A cherry tree in splendid bloom.
And people. Faces from every land,
identical in other cities,
virtually interchangeable
since the indelible imprint
conspire to make us look alike,
dress alike
listen to the same music,
many eat different ethnic foods,
activities of individuals
determined by their prosperity.

Treasure Hunter

I wake each morning
just after sunrise
sweeping my metal detector
back and forth,
hand shovel, swag net,
always ready
for the big find
that's never there.
The punk kid
goes out on his surfboard
every morning and insults me:
"Hey Pop. Find any treasure?
Ha, ha."
One day
I'll find something great,
maybe a rolex watch
and show him.

America Unfurled

Americans learned early
how to steal land from others
from British colonists
who quickly evicted the Dutch,
unwilling to let foreigners
occupy the tempting frontier
of the new world,
which they wanted for their own
without the faintest idea
of the size of the vast continent.

As more colonists arrived
they settled, needed more room,
then began the long usurpation
of Native American lands,
taking when strong,
negotiating when weak,
a pattern cleverly employed
until the colonies were strong enough
to dispute ownership with the French
and forcibly expel them.

As the colonies flourished
the British Empire grew,
spreading across the world
by conquest, trade, or both
a lesson to watchful colonists
conveniently gifted
with the same genetic urge
to acquire land from others
on some occasions peacefully,
but almost always by war.

When the great separation began

between colonies and motherland
the King and Parliament were shocked
by the revolutionary fervor
of the graduate students
of advanced acquisition,
who thoroughly understood
that when someone grabs illegally
they establish a precedent
for others to grab illegally.

Thus began the great leap forward
as founders of the new nation
quickly consolidated the gains
from the recent revolution,
digested that they had defeated
the strongest empire in the world,
which sent a jolt of confidence
coursing through the covetous veins
of land hungry occidentals
willing to kill for their own farms.

The snatching of other people's lands,
became the object of existence
for all those able to snatch
a new homestead, a new life.
And always distantly unseen
the men of wealth and hunger,
whose only mantra was more, more,
manipulated the masses
with pronouncements from Washington
like 'Manifest Destiny'.

So we got rid of the foreigners,
Russians, French, the Spanish,
so we could concentrate efforts
on removing the Indians
who interfered with expansion
preventing exploration,

mining, farming, trade, settlements,
constricting acquisition of more,
so obstacles of progress
had to be eliminated.

Our fundamental greed
brought irreconcilable groups,
Northern industrial magnates,
Southern agricultural barons,
into inevitable conflict,
over who would rule the new empire.
When compromise was exhausted
they resolved their differences
in a bloody civil war
that ended Southern gentry rule.

Control of the future
of the partially battered land
liberally decided
by the use of gunpowder
the new lords of profit
knew few restrictions
in using the economy
to fund the fundamental urge
to acquire the land of others,
more by war then peacefully.

Reconstruction in the South
raised a new class to wealth, power,
then infected them with hunger
for the lands of others,
defeating the Sioux, Apaches,
until there was only one rule
from the Atlantic Ocean
to the Pacific Ocean
with increased appetite for more.

In our first offshore venture

we quickly assaulted
the crumbling Spanish Empire,
establishing our empire
in the Caribbean,
then in the Pacific.
And the new captive people
needed the benefit
of democracy,
enforced by the gun.

So we surprised the old dogs
in Europe and Asia
by displaying our power.
But they knew we were children.
When they exhausted themselves
in the biggest war ever,
they thought they outsmarted us
in the treaty of Versailles,
yet they never realized
we learned to fight a world war.

The 'Great Depression' shattered lives
of millions of Americans
who couldn't drink legally
to forget their troubles
courtesy of the Volstead Act
that gave birth to organized crime
illicitly providing,
the booze that everyone craved,
generating enough wealth
to corrupt our government.

Yet the long soup kitchen lines
of the desperately hungry
dominated the media
and Hollywood pictures,
but concealed new factories
that began to produce

steel, oil, automobiles,
while our growing agriculture
began to feed a starving world,
adding to our wealth and power.

The seekers of expansion
ordered their armies to march
into weaker countries
that could not resist
modern war machines.
Soon the world was engulfed
in devastating conflict
as invading hordes
ravaged the conquered,
looting captive nations.

Some foreign autocrats
did not realize
industrious America
created a mighty system
to produce massive amounts
for the necessities of war.
One peaceful December morning
when we were bombed into action
we quickly built ships, planes, tanks, guns
that defeated our enemies.

After a few bloody years
we inherited the earth,
inhabitants exhausted
by ravages of modern war.
Our legions camped in other lands
ensuring the new order
of economic dominance
would not know interference
as our sales of oil, steel, cars
did not have competitors.

So we rebuilt Japan
and rebuilt Germany,
challenged surly soviets,
reveling in the profits
 of glorious victory
as the dollar ruled the world.
When millions of soldiers
came back from World War II,
factories closed, they went to college
and became the middle class.

The cunning lords of profit
driven by relentless greed
successfully removed
those who would fight the bosses
for a fair share of earnings,
replaced them with a new class
that sat behind desks, computers
and became so prosperous
they would not risk losing all
in an idealistic fight.

Within established 'Cold War' rules
that ensured it wouldn't become hot
we sent the legions to Vietnam
to preserve democracy.
As our youth were bleeding, dying
in a far off Asian land,
youth and supporters at home
vigorously protested the war,
alienating the true blue,
bitterly dividing the nation.

The 'Great Schism' distracted us
from innovative business deals
closing most of our factories
that cost too much to retool,
paid our workers too much

and offshored them abroad
where they didn't pay taxes
and paid low wages
abandoning America
to make greater profits.

The protests of the Vietnam War
that divided the nation
made the lords of profit rejoice.
Instead of an aware people
following the affairs of state,
the media told the nation
we had become two opposed groups
each with their own agenda,
far more important to them
then the fate of our country.

Many citizens believed
republicans or democrats
knew what was best for our land.
Each party had mouthpieces,
media propagandists,
who told us what we should know.
They weren't allowed to tell us
the 1% hired both sides
to keep us polarized
while the rich grew richer.

The evidence of betrayal
of the American people
is carefully concealed
so we argue with each other
as we grow poorer and poorer,
our land grows weaker and weaker,
since the rapacious 1%
are no longer invested
in the future of our land,
while their wealth is in other lands.

Our tragedy, America,
is that an indifferent few
determine the fate of many,
abandoning our tomorrow
by amalgamating our wealth
while impoverishing our land,
eroding our security
as we face many foreign foes,
while we do not realize
our empire is crumbling.

The Park

People dogwalking,
sitting on the grass
eating, reading, texting,
comfortable and relaxed,
as if it's not America
ravaged by Covid-19,
angrily divided
by political factions
that prefer collapse
to compromise.

Armaments

Once when I was a boy
I asked my grandfather:
"What is that burned thing
that hangs over the fireplace?"
"Asadi," that he only called me
when father was away.
"That is the FIM – 92 Stinger,
a man portable, surface to air missile,
that allowed the Mujahadeen…
You remember what the Mujahadeen were?"
"Yes, Grandfather. Holy warriors
who defeated the godless Russians."
"Good boy. You will get a treat for that.
I myself shot down…
Eight helicopters
with this wonderful weapon."
"Do our holy warriors
use them today
to fight the Americans?"
"No, little lion.
Our friends in Pakistan and Iran
give us new weapons
to defeat the invaders.
Allah willing."

Continuation

The life of the city
relies on
continuation
No matter who dies
things will go on,
as long as the wheels
that make things run
keep turning.

Clinic

After showing I.D.,
insurance card,
I'm busy
filling out forms;
name, address, age,
a zillion health questions,
page after page
of personal info,
race, creed…
Well not creed.
There are still some limits
to hospital intrusions,
as long as you can pay.

The waiting room is packed.
An hour later the nurse announces:
"Sorry. The doctor can't see
anyone else today.
please make a new appointment."
I trudge to the desk
get a new date
and on the long trip home
find myself hoping
I don't have to do
the paperwork again.

Different Customs

I walk the cooling streets
and no longer see
the thighs of summer
tantalizingly displayed
in very short shorts,
privileged young women
totally unaware
they would be arrested,
harshly punished
by the morals police
in countries that object
to showing female flesh.

Strange Surroundings

I have always lived
in alien enclaves.
never taking root
no matter how long I stayed
in one place
long enough to belong,
my distance from others
engraved in my soul,
that for some reason,
cause, curse, inheritance,
coincidental as existence
I am as temporary
as a gust of wind,
though I move slowly enough
that I don't blow away,
in an instant.

I began
like so many others
without knowledge, experience,
just need
urgent appetite
to be fed, held, soothed
in the strange new world,
having been abruptly removed
from conception chamber
where all needs
were gratified
without thought, question,
everything flowed
as I wanted,
warm, comfortable, secure.

Then disruption.
Demands to vacate the premises
I resisted with all my might,
not wanting to leave
home.
Intrusive hands
forced me out,
yanked me into the cold,
wrapped me in garments,
but it wasn't the same,
put me on someone's warmth
but it wasn't the same,
There was nothing else
and for the moment
my ordeal was over.
I slept.

For many years
I worked and gave of my soul
to homeless families with children,
most of them surgically removed
from the rest of society,
placed in isolated hotels
in unwelcoming neighborhoods,
identities horribly subtracted
by callous government agencies,
abandoned by those who should help
who escape responsibility
because the homeless are transformed
into non-citizens,
arbitrarily deprived of their rights,
more vulnerable then most of us,
and the children feel the disconnect
between them and humanity.

After Decline

Life has become so complex
in the good old U.S.A.
that the average citizen
can no longer understand
the issues that divide us.
Just as we get a handle
on the biggest current problems,
Covid-19, immigration,
shutdown of the government,
disasters suddenly happen,
wild fires, floods, hurricanes,
further eroding the fabric
of a struggling society
slowly being overwhelmed
by the conflicting demands
to maintain our fraying country.

Whose Country is it?

I   Is America crazier
than in the past?
Was anything crazier
than the Civil War?
Americans killing Americans
for who would rule the country,
Northern Industrial Magnates
or Southern Agricultural barons?

And many of the men were told
they were fighting about slavery,
even though it affected few of them.
Were we more moral then?
Dumber? Definitely Not!
More gullible? Maybe.
Information was different then
It moved slowly
from points of origin,
without video, audio,
just the printed word,
black and white illustrations.

II   Not many protested the Spanish-American War
when we stole a senor empire
from an attenuated European power
and moved onto the world stage
with the 'Great White Fleet'
sailing the seven seas,
announcing to the old empires
a new player in the game,
not reluctant to project power,
snatch Hawaii, then Guam

        declaring to Pacific nations,
        'we're here to stay.'

III   Teddy mediated the Russo-Japanese War
        that furthered Russian resentment of us
        and birthed Japanese hatred
        when we didn't give them enough
        for defeating the moldy Russian bear.
        But our leaders learned enough
        to build a bigger role
        in international affairs,
        even though we didn't always know
        what we were doing
        and were often outsmarted
        by the European old dogs.

IV   So World War I went on
        and on and we finally intervened,
        turned the tide against weary Germany,
        then were completely outmaneuvered
        after the armistice was declared
        by the cunning French,
        the ruthless British
        and got little from the settlement,
        but started the League of Nations,
        an impotent body that couldn't compel
        anyone from rivaling anyone else,
        couldn't alleviate suffering,
        couldn't prevent war,
        poverty, hunger, disease,
        the ills that beset the world.

V   The Great Depression struck most of us.,
        except those wealthy enough
        to survive all disasters
        and they profited mightily,

feasting in splendor
while millions dined at soup kitchens.
Yet unbeknownst to the public
a mighty empire was stirring,
getting richer, more powerful,
ready to replace tired empires
once the aggressors
were totally defeated
and we inherited the Earth.

Social Malfeasance

A sudden news bulletin:
'Shooter at Texas High School'.
We look at the news channel
and see a familiar sight;
kids coming out in panic,
hands over their heads
to show they're are not armed.
Police escort them out of range
until the situation's clear.
SWAT arrives, moves purposefully
to the uninviting doors
that may conceal instant death.
They enter, some scared, some psyched,
urgent to end the danger.
After killing and wounding some,
the shooter escapes
ensuring the government
the expense of a trial,
unless the police kill him,
or he kills himself,
another testament
to the indiscriminate right
for the disturbed to acquire guns.

Innovation

We have been trained to accept
the marvels of technology,
camping out in rain or snow
for the latest IPhone, IPad,
following social media
that subtlety or brazenly
assaults the minds of our youngsters,
mostly hidden from adults,
manipulated by tv,
absorbed by FOX News, CNN,
too busy to monitor kids
separated from parents,
another alienated group
further shattering the family,
the fundamental unit
that maintains civilization,
arbitrarily altered
for the comfort and convenience
of the exploitative 1%.

O Joyous Day

The word spread like lightning –
The Americans are gone!
We fired our AK-47's in the air
and cheered in celebration.
Then we went to their hanger
where they left behind
rows of helicopters.
My eyes grew wide
at our new found treasures
and Batoor nudged me:
"We are on camera.
Look natural."
I thanked him silently,
then thanked Allah
for the wonderful weapons
that will help us
bring Sharia to the world.

Our Land, Lost

Ernest voices tell us daily
what's wrong with the opposition.
Rabid voices tell us daily
what's wrong with the opposition.
Some prefer the righteous left.
Some prefer the ranting right.
The American tradition
that we always are divided,
save for brief patriotic wars,
that allow the owners of our land
to further accumulate wealth,
letting paltry sums trickle down
to the dwindling middle class,
keeping them content,
while the 99%
are distracted by Congress
with sincere pronouncements
they are diligently working
for the interests of the people.

Imperial Reach

Superficial commentators
try to alarm us
that China is turning inwards,
rejecting the English language,
isolating itself,
when in reality
their growing economic might
buys entry in many countries
establishing a power base
throughout the Pacific region,
in Asia, in Europe,
even South America
and some of us understand
they are not withdrawing,
just replacing America
as custodians of the world.

Democracy Wounded

In the not too distant past
many Americans
had comfortable lives,
more than any other people
in history.

There was always a struggle
between haves and have nots,
but enough was shared
that local protests
were the order of the day
rather then revolution.

But the lords of profit
who never have enough
changed our nation,
sending factories abroad
ending the blue collar class
that moderated the rich
by their willingness to fight
for fair treatment.

So our industry
was replaced with technology
and average citizens
could not master the new way
and their confidence dwindled,
they accepted service jobs.

The lords of profit smiled
because they removed resistance
to the new economics,
plenty for the few,
little trickling down
for the needs of many.

Selfish is

Tax the rich was often heard
in Babylon, Athens, Rome,
many other empires,
indifferently ignored
until it led to unrest,
then brutally suppressed,
while one man feasts in a palace,
another starves in a hovel
and the rich always believe
this is condition normal.

Fake News

Events in the world
grow more chaotic
as authoritarian states
exert more control
over people seeking freedom.
Military confrontation
grows more dangerous
as weapons of mass destruction
proliferate
accompanied by
provocative missile launches,
cyberwarfare,
subversion of other nations,
insanely regarded
in America
as situation normal,
while Mother Nature prepares
to harshly terminate
intrusive life forms
that disrupt the balance
of normal existence.

Persistence

My grandfather
fought the Russians
like his holy warrior brothers
and never lost hope,
despite the helicopters and tanks
that killed so many,
so many innocent
women and children,
destroyed our mosques,
flaunted their godless ways
making whores of our women,
teaching our children
to deny the true faith,
until that blessed day
they accepted defeat,
left our battered country
by the Friendship Bridge,
faces like stone
as the vanquished departed.

My father fought the Northern Alliance,
our former fellow Mujahedeen
who refused to accept the true law,
led by the Tajik leader
the Lion of Fanjshir',
fighters from other ethnic groups,
perverted by exposure
to decadent European ways,
trying to form a multi-ethnic state
under a moderate form of Islam.
The deceivers of the people
denied that Sharia welcomes all,
until they were finally defeated
and accepted the rule of the Taliban.

Now my sons fight the Americans
who invaded to destroy al qaeda
after the 9/11 attack
that thrilled all islam.
They do not understand
that people of the true faith
will never submit to infidels

and will resist them to the death,
no matter how long it takes,
ten, twenty, thirty years,
until we establish
the pure rule of Sharia.
God is great.

Gun Crazy

What a country!
Mass shootings murder our children,
but we don't stop kids from getting guns.
Massacres in nightclubs and stores
are quickly forgotten
when a new shooting occurs.
It's more important
the NRA asserts,
to protect constitutional rights
than to ban the insane,
than to ban criminals
from acquiring assault rifles
to use in public places
on innocent citizens,
since the second amendment
doesn't discriminate
against who should bear arms.

Abandonment

My grandfather worked for the Russians
who paid him enough
to feed his family.
When the Taliban defeated
the godless dogs
they shot my grandfather.
Just before he died
he told my father:
'Do not work for the infidel
for they will betray you'.
When the Americans
came to Afghanistan
I told my sons :
'Do not work for them,
for they will betray you'.
One son was a translator.
Another a military contractor.
They both explained:
'It's the only way
to feed our families'.
When the Taliban defeated
the infidel Americans
they promised to save my sons,
but they abandoned them.
Now I tell their children:
'Never trust an infidel'.

Extinction Path

We do not go
into the streets
the way we used to,
fearing the virus
evolving faster
than our mindsets
dealing with it.
The plague on our land
dividing us,
as everything else
divides us,
revealing our failures,
as many prefer
a million deaths
to compromise.

Park Sights

An overcast September day
in lingering summer.
As we walk through Central Park,
in concrete and glass New York City,
it begins to rain
and people start to leave,
except dedicated bikers,
peddling fast or slow.
We decide to wait awhile
hoping the rain will stop
and are suddenly rewarded
with the incredible sight
of a large hawk
swooping between the trees,
snatching an unwary squirrel,
carrying him off in his talons
for dinner alfresco,
an abrupt reminder
the park is not as tame
as urbanites assume.

Know Thy Deceivers

Climate change disinformation
has been promoted daily
by right-wing media outlets,
politicians and polluters,
who oppose climate action
to maintain and preserve
fossil fuel status quo,
mostly motivated
by greed and ignorance.
The rabid climate denials
demonstrate how a few
are misleading many,
in anti-climate conspiracy
to convince the world at large
the earth is not being destroyed,
the future is not endangered
in the ruthless quest for profits.

Loss

I watched on tv
as a squad of Marines
carried my fathers' coffin
from the plane to the van
for transport to Arlington.
The President, First Lady,
generals, admirals,
respectfully watched
the solemn ceremony.
I couldn't help crying
even though I didn't know
which coffin was his.
What I did know,
he wasn't coming home
from Afghanistan.
I couldn't help wondering
why they didn't take care of him.

Priorities

Whoever values art
will be captivated
when a major collection
of museum quality
comes up for auction.
Peddlers consider it
a defining moment
in the art market
for indulgent spenders
who would rather buy pictures
for millions of dollars
than help the needy.

War Power

The President Bush
started the war.
The President Obama
continued the war.
The President Trump
continued the war,
then he talked to us
without the false government
and the people knew
that we would win.
The President Biden
continued the war,
then panicked when he knew
that he would lose,
so he rushed his troops out
leaving most of the traitors
for Taliban justice.

Replace Humans

Driver assistance systems
that can steer, accelerate
and brake on its own
drove into fire trucks, police cars,
emergency vehicles
and were in other accidents.
Though autonomous cars
are supposed to replace drivers,
they are instructed
to keep their hand on the wheel.
People being people,
they often neglect
this safety feature.
In one crash the driver was drunk.
Another driver in the back seat
was watching a movie.
Some fall asleep at the wheel.
We need better A.I.
to improve safe driving
and get rid of human drivers,
the cause of countless accidents,
as soon as possible.

Homeless in Paradise

The price of gas went up again.
I couldn't afford to fill the tank,
so I sold the old Toyota.
The bus doesn't run too often.
I got to the supermarket late
for my job as a bag boy
and the manager let me go.
The landlord raised the rent again.
My Social Security check
isn't enough for food and rent.
Florida's warm most of the time
so I'll try to sleep on the beach,
unless there's a hurricane,
then I don't know what I'll do.
I won't go to a nursing home.
I'll just live as long as I can.

Endurance

Many years ago
when our imam was young,
full of fire in the faith,
the godless Russians came,
invading the mosque,
searching for Mujahadeen
the imam tried to stop them
from defiling the holy place.
They hit him with gun butts,
knocked him down, kicked him,
but he knew they were coming
and sent our men away
so they could fight another day.

Our imam is old now,
but still full of fire in the faith,
so when the Americans came
searching for our holy warriors
he tried to stop them
from defiling a holy place.
They pushed him aside,
but he knew they were coming
and sent our men away
so they could fight another day.

Madness Revealed

Condos keep going up.
People keep flooding in.
Everyone wants to live here.
Before the real estate bubble burst
in 2008, they were so crazy
they bought future condos
on empty land.
A lot of them lost everything,
but the still keep coming,
crowding out native Floridians,
some families here since the 1920s.
Soon there'll be so many condos
crammed onto the shore line
that if they're not blown away
by a giant hurricane,
they'll sink into the sea
from the rising tides.

Afghan Climate

A decline in spring rains
affected most of the country,
so farmers and herders
who rely on rain to grow crops,
water their flocks,
will not provide food
to the war torn nation,
where three fourths of the people
work in agriculture,
as frequent and severe
droughts, floods, desertification,
may be calamities,
while the Taliban
are more concerned
with removing women's pictures
from public billboards,
than addressing climate change.

Tourist Drudge

I work as a maid
at the old hotel
on the beach.
Despite the talk of Covid
the hotel's full of tourists,
mostly from Orlando.
Most of them are fat
and they're very cheap,
only leaving 2 or 3 dollar tips
for cleaning their mess.
Me, Jim and the kid are healthy,
but Jim won't let us get vaccine,
and Covid is spreading in Florida,
specially in Volusia county
where we live.
I'm not against vaccine like Jim,
but I still don't like it,
yet I don't wanta get
what them folks from Orlando
may be bringing.

Imprecation

I curse the Americans.
They lured my beautiful daughter
to work at their embassy
as a translator.
I warned her it was dangerous
and not our custom
for a woman to work for foreigners,
but she was happy
and they promised
to pay for her education.
So I ignored my misgivings.
Then the Taliban came to Kabul
and they closed the embassy,
ran away like craven dogs
and left my daughter behind.
The Taliban came for her
and I tried to protect her,
but they beat me
and took her away,
my beautiful daughter
who I'll never see again.
I curse the Americans.

Surfs Up

Chet and I watch the old guy
carry his longboard into the water.
He takes a long time to paddle out,
then waits and waits but never rides.
We don't get much of a ride
on the tiny waves,
but its better then nothing
and we feel like surfers.

Chet thinks the old guy is a real surfer
and he doesn't bother with the dinky waves.
We talk about him a lot.
One morning we looked around
and he wasn't there.
All we saw was a fin
slowly moving away.

Triumph

It's not a rumor.
It's true.
The infidel Americans
are finally departing,
defeated
by the holy warriors
as we defeated
the infidel Russians.
Despite their tanks, drones,
helicopters,
the vaunted technology
that can never conquer
men of faith.
Now that we have our country
we will use it as our base
to bring Sharia
to the entire world.
God is great.

Beach Din

The beach is crowded.
Cars fill up all the spaces.
Umbrellas and tents shield many
from the hot summer sun.
People are throwing footballs,
baseballs, frisbees,
kicking soccer balls,
ridding boogie boards,
crowding the shoreline
with busy play.
Three children sit in a tidal pool
whispering together,
enrapt in a child's game
and no one notices
the quiet place on the beach

Afghan Pullout

The Taliban celebrated
independence from America
after twenty years of war
with gunfire in Kabul streets.
President Biden declared:
'leaving or escalating
was the only choice'.
The chaotic departure
before the Taliban takeover
was dismissed by the President
as necessary to end
the 'forever war',
that left thousands of allies
to the mercy of the Taliban
who could have been saved
with an orderly withdrawal,
following the tradition
of abandoning allies
when we couldn't win the war.

Ersatz Surfers

My buddy and I
go to the beach
weekend mornings
wearing wetsuits,
carrying longboards
and never go in the water.
We try to avoid real surfers
who make fun of us.
But we really don't care
as long as we're chick magnets,
attracting young tourist women
not here long enough
to find out we're phonies.

Dedicated

The infidel Americans
were shocked at how fast
we captured Kabul.
They warned us:
'Don't let ISIS come back'.
As if they were ever gone.
The stupid Westerners
do not understand
that holy warriors
and holy martyrs
are the same faith.

Lost Flock

I wake each morning
at first light,
stretch my wings,
fly to water's edge
seeking food.
Humans are everywhere
walking, running,
riding wheeled things.
It never feels right
moving alone.
I vaguely remember
when there were many Sandpipers
and we'd fly in unison,
move up and down with the tide
in unison.
We did everything together
and it was good.
Now my wings grow tired.
I can't find much food
when the waves go out.
I'm always hungry.
Soon I will fly no more
and I will be forgotten
as my flock is forgotten.

Mega-Corp Abuse

Apple announced changes to Iphones
to spot child pornography
and added a feature
for parents to be flagged
when children receive nude photos.
Apple assured users
that privacy is protected
so sexual predators
can continue to use the internet
without consequences.
Some cybersecurity experts,
concerned that surveillance technology
could be exploited by law enforcement
to apprehend criminals,
believe the constitution
protects pedophiles,
as well as other citizens
from government intrusion.

Malice Aforethought

Some claim that deniers
are dangerous liars
trying to confuse us
about something that happened
by telling us it didn't.
Now all kinds of psych folks
explain why they do it
psychologically,
presenting the motives,
attention getting behavior,
self enhancing ego trip,
the reasons go on and on.
So when someone asserts
we didn't land on the moon
it's rejecting reality,
or doubting the government.
But in the end result
doesn't do too much harm,
it's science or fiction
that won't damage many lives.
However. When you say
the Holocaust didn't happen
you are excusing
an insane regime
that built concentration camps,
then murdered millions
they thought undesirable,
therefore opening the doors
for other lunatics
to target certain groups
for elimination,
ending civilization.

Ode to Texas

The ravenous horde
of land usurpers
took advantage
of Mexican tolerance
for Yankee settlers
to steal as much as they could
from a sovereign nation.
Then they refused to obey
their host government,
so a punitive force
destroyed resistance
at the Alamo,
the dead were proclaimed heroes
and remember the 'you know what'
led to illegal rebellion,
then American invaders
seized Mexican territory.

Today when some folk object
to Texas banning abortion,
restricting voting rights,
denying the holocaust,
we fervently hope
reasonable people
will strenuously protest
when a rabid group
wants to change the state flag
to the swastika.

Stampede

I joined the panicky horde
struggling to get to the airfield
and we all keep trying
while many are dying,
but we must risk all
no matter the cost.
Who doesn't get away
will surely be killed
by the righteous Taliban
for serving the Americans.

War For Whom?

Murmurs of another defeat
after a hasty retreat
from untamed Afghanistan
resonate across the land,
as ponderous legislators
prepare their investigation:
'Why we lost the Forever War'.
What they won't reveal to us
is the profits big business made
supplying the needs of warfare,
rewards the military earned,
promotions over 20 years,
at least Army, Air Force, Marines,
just the Navy was neglected
from landlocked Afghanistan,
another war they couldn't enjoy.
Those who did not benefit
from the foreign expedition
were the American public
of dwindling opportunity,
diminishing rights, poverty,
while the 1% consume us.

Spector Weapons

Ghost guns are spreading
throughout New York City,
firearms without serial numbers
assembled from kits bought online
from gun manufacturers
seeking a bigger market
to expand profits,
so felons, the mentally ill,
can acquire guns
without the inconvenience
of going to the store.

Audiology Department

The waiting room is crowded.
The nurse comes for the patient,
calling his name loudly,
knowing from experience
to raise her voice for those
here for a hearing test.

Blindness

Disasters ravage our land.
Many people die.
Billions of dollars
are lost in damages.
The country is disrupted.
Despite obvious threats
to future stability
it's more important to the rich
to preserve their privileges,
maintain their profits,
than save Americans
from threatened destruction.

Ignored

My stubborn son
refused to listen to me.
'Don't worry, Papa.
The Americans promised
to take us with them
when they leave'.
My headstrong daughter
refused to listen to me:
'Don't worry, Papa,
I'll be alright
working for the Americans.
They'll be here for a long time
and it's a great opportunity
for me to have a career
as a translator.
The Americans promised
to take us with them
if they left.
Surely we can trust them
not to abandon us'.

Servitude

Some elected officials
voted into office
to serve the people
are obedient servants
to the fossil fuel industry
and refuse to acknowledge
the disasters that get worse,
fires, floods, storms, droughts
are due to climate change
destroying our country
faster and faster,
while the fuel lobby
denies the rest of us
resources to save
the declining environment,
their master's profits
far more important
then our well-being.

Orders

'Don't worry, Bibi',
my American advisor
sincerely promised
as we fought the Taliban.
'If things get worse
I'll get you out.
We've been through too much
for me to abandon you'.
Then he got his orders
to pack up and get out
the next morning.
'What about me?
You promised to save me.
Now you're leaving me'.
'I've got my orders', Bibi.
I'll try to get you out,
but I've got to obey orders.
I told the Lieutenant
and he promised to help.
We'll try our best,
but we've got to go'.

National Interests

Corporate America
sits in their boardrooms
determining policies
to increase their profits,
a consistent process
that overshadows
many other concerns.
The recent initiative
to increase taxes
that actually aren't paid
will easily be deflected
by indentured legislators
eager to do the bidding
of remote masters,
rewarding obedience
with position, power, comforts,
as the growing separation
between haves and nave nots
is carefully engineered
preserving the privileged,
deaccessing the people.

Separate

Outside the sheltered,
bland painted halls,
the schools I attended
were too new,
too public
for ivy covered walls.

Aquatic Afflictions

Recreational boating boomed
during the pandemic
with many new boaters
taking to the water
without knowing what they were doing,
speeding recklessly,
endangering themselves, others,
crashing, getting lost,
running aground,
then calling for help
from the understaffed
overworked nautical authorities.

Opportunist

I spied for the Russians
for nine prosperous years
until they were defeated
by the Mujahadeen.
I concealed my wealth
carefully from my neighbors
and my family ate better,
not enough to arouse suspicion.
I didn't trust the Northern Alliance
not to betray me to the Taliban,
so I worked the family plot
and didn't think I'd spy again.
Then the naive Americans came
and trusted just about anyone
who said they'd help them.
We got rich for twenty years
selling out the Taliban,
then the Americans
suddenly got up and left.
I don't know how my family
will get out of Afghanistan
with our fortune.

The Eyes of Texas…

The Governor of Texas
forbidding censorship,
signed a bill, banning
social media platforms
from removing posts
because of political views.
Under the new rules
Facebook and Twitter
can't remove or moderate
a users post.
Private citizens can sue
social media companies
for violating the law
as long as they live in Texas.
Yahoo.

Dimming Calls

We once had great flocks
and swarmed the fields
ignoring the scarecrows.
Some of us would fall
from the farmer's shotgun,
but we ate.
Then the big machines came.
They cut down our trees
so we had nowhere to nest.
They always guarded the fields,
even at night,
so we could not feed.
With no place left to live
we came to the cities,
but there wasn't food for the flock
so most of us died.
We flew to warm places,
small towns by the beach,
where there's not enough food
and many crows will die,
but some of us may survive.

Veterans Care

Using office software,
satellite maps,
encrypted messaging apps,
a concerned veterans group
tried to get Americans
and Afghan allies
safely out of Kabul
before the Taliban got them.
They acted like guides
using their cellphones
provide the best routes
to avoid Taliban checkpoints
through overlooked alleys,
sometimes sewage canals,
until they reached the airfield
and were finally admitted,
while thousands were left behind.
There was no information
why the C.I.A., Pentagon, White House
weren't using the same tools
to save people's lives.

Decayed Conditions

We used to go to the beach a lot
and the kids loved feeding the seagulls
who'd hover on the air,
almost on top of them
and catch bread crusts,
but there aren't many left.
When we go now
it's always crowded.
We drive a long way
to find a parking space.
There's always people
playing ball,
playing radios,
so it's not peaceful.
Most of the time
we can't go in the water,
rip tides, jellyfish, sharks.
Florida's not the same.
We may as well stay home
and watch tv.

Interpreter Escape

I was a 'terp' with the Marines.
I had a green card
and was visiting my family
when the Taliban took Kabul.
I was scared they'd find me
and execute me.
I took off my American clothes,
put on traditional Afghan garb,
a long shirt and turban
and my mother hid my passport
until we got to the airport.
My brother pushed me through the crowd
I showed my passport to the Marines,
they pulled me over the wire
and I was safe.
Now I worry about my family
and thousands of my countrymen
who didn't escape.

Big Wave Dreams

I go out each morning
and practice what I learned
from videos the night before.
I paddle out like all surfers,
the only difference
the waves are too small
for more then a short ride.
But I'm mastering technique,
so when I go to Hawaii
I'll ride the waves like a pro surfer.

Politics Agonistes

I worked for the Governor
for less than three months.
I tried to make him understand
that all the condos on the coast
were consuming the water table,
producing excessive waste
overwhelming the environment.
Yet people keep moving in
without the resources to support them.
He dismissed my warnings,
called them alarmist,
so I quit.
I can't be a science advisor
if he doesn't believe in science.

Airborne

We landed at Kabul airport –
we don't jump much anymore,
too big a target
floating down slowly
for the guys with AK-47's.
They told us our mission:
'To protect Americans
and other evacuees
from ISIS, al qaeda,
especially ISIS.
and the Taliban'.
But I can't tell them apart.
They all look the same to me.
So I'll waste anyone
who points a weapon at me.

Aging

I run each morning
though I'm slower then I used to be.
There are only a few people at dawn
and none run as far as me,
all the way to Flagler Avenue.
I have trouble finishing
the rest of the way on the sand.
Soon I'll have to turn back earlier.
I don't know how long I'll keep going,
but I'll run on New Smyrna Beach
each morning until I die.

Failing Wings

I am old and tired.
Soon I won't be able to fly,
then I'll die.
There used to be many Grackles
soaring and displaying
in fields and towns
before humans drove us away
from feeding grounds.
So we went to the shore
where for a while
we entertained humans
walking fast on our long legs,
flashing our lustrous tails.
But there are fierce competitors,
gulls, pigeons, crows
who drive us away.
No one notices as we disappear
and it's as if we never were,
for no one ever sees
a dead Grackle.

Do Gooder

They make fun of me,
call me 'the turtle lady',
even tease how I walk,
'slow like a turtle',
just because I ask them
not to disturb the nests
in nesting season
and put their lights out at night
that face the beach,
which disorients hatchlings
who wander inland and die
of dehydration, predation.
You'd think people would care
about helpless creatures,
but I'm still shocked
when I find out they don't.

Tourist Sight

If I want to eat
I have to stand still for hours
in the shallow water of the river
waiting for fish to swim by,
then swoosh, I dip my neck
my sharp beak impales fish
and I eat.
But the boats come closer
and I have to fly,
but it takes time to take off,
 not like smaller birds,
so it's always dangerous.
There used to be lots of us
up and down the river.
Now I hang out on the dock
and humans feed me,
some throw things at me,
make weird sounds at me:
'look at the pretty heron',
before I can fly away.

At Last

What a glorious day!
Thanks to Allah.
The Americans are gone.
What my imam taught me
has proven true:
'America talks righteously
but really fights for gain.
When things grow difficult
they slink away like dogs,
as they always do,
abandoning collaborators
to face justice.
They cannot understand
twenty years of war
is as nothing
to holy warriors
who will fight one hundred years
to bring Sharia
to a needy world.

Depleted Waterway

My mate and I
have been hungry too long.
There's no more food in the river.
The lakes are too crowded.
So we flew to the ocean
and tried to find food on the beach.
The water goes back and forth,
so there's no time to hunt.
The humans keep chasing us.
There are no trees or bushes
for shade from the sun
as we look for fish.
I don't know if we'll survive
this harsh place,
but there's nowhere else
for Egrets to go.

www.ingramcontent.com/pod-product-compliance
Lightning Source LLC
Chambersburg PA
CBHW070450050426
42451CB00015B/3421